FruitArt

Author: **Lannice Snyman**

Photographer: **Malcolm Dare**

Designer & Stylist: **Brita du Plessis**

Lannice Snyman Publishers

FruitArt

'A table, a chair, a bowl of fruit and a violin;
what else does a man need to be happy?'

Albert Einstein

ACKNOWLEDGEMENTS

LIM for their unique range of earthy crockery and place mats that lend the photographs a distinctly modern African feel.

HEARTWORKS for the stunning handmade platter from Mustardseed & Moonshine.

ANOUSCHKA VENTER for all her hard work handling the production.

PIXEL FOUNDRY for the use of their studios, kitchen, lights and eager staff, always willing to act as tasters.

First published in 2006 by Lannice Snyman Publishers
PO Box 26344, Hout Bay 7872, South Africa
E-mail: lannice@lannicesnyman.com
Website: www.lannicesnyman.com

Author: Lannice Snyman
Photographer & Digital Retoucher: Malcolm Dare
Photographic Assistant: Matthys van Lill
Author's Photograph: Muriel Rossi
Designer & Stylist: Brita du Plessis
Finished Art: Tanja Schultz
Proofreader: Glynne Newlands
Make-up: Jenny Fraser and Teri Lynn Gardner

Printed and bound in Singapore by Tien Wah Press Pte Ltd

IBSN 0-620-36104-2
EAN/BARCODE 9780620361040

Contents

'Life without love is like a tree without blossoms or fruit.'

Kahlil Gibran

Introduction

'Live each season as it passes; breathe the air,
drink the drink, taste the fruit, and resign yourself to the influences of each.'

Henry David Thoreau

In the grand scheme of things, fruit is pivotal to health and happiness and, as a result, creates harmony in the home and world peace. Alright, that may be stretching things a bit, but you get my drift.

Fruit's first claim to fame was as an object of seduction. And nothing much has changed since Eve tempted Adam with that apple. Just as I was seduced by Malcolm Dare's extraordinary collection of fruit-with-the-female-form photographs which triggered this unique book.

Like life, *Fruit Art* seems to have happened while we were doing something else, as we opted for a freestyle approach to the project and didn't box ourselves in with deadlines and time schedules. We pleased ourselves first and foremost and, accordingly, hope to please our readers. The result is an inspired melding of creativity, where freshness and immediacy are given full reign.

Fruit Art promises to raise eyebrows, satisfy the senses, and thrill everyone who adores beautiful books, sexy recipes, photographs that push the creativity envelope, and edgy styling. It's a must-have item if you love cooking (but don't have too much time to spend doing it) or for a gift for a special friend. Either way, it's a book that deserves to be treasured.

When deciding on which fruit to select for *Fruit Art*, we chose the obvious varieties, ones that add a little sweetness to our menus and are happy in dishes both sweet and savoury. Adding tomatoes and avocados to the line-up allowed more breadth of vision and rounded out the recipes to see you from breakfast, through tea time, to soups, salads and an array of main dishes that feature seafood, chicken, pork, lamb and beef. Not to mention a clutch of delish desserts and other after-dinner delectations.

Luscious fruit begs to be eaten fresh and fast – at the peak of ripeness and without overmuch tampering by the cook. Our recipes aim to fulfil these principles: nothing too time-consuming, plates that are not over-presented, and ingredient lists that err on the side of brevity. Most importantly, these recipes respect good ingredients and their relationship with each other, and are mindful of the limited time we have to spend in the kitchen.

We avoided the temptation to preach about the whys and wherefores of growing, harvesting, buying and storing fruit. It is useful to know, however, that while texture and colour improves after some fruit has been harvested, most fruit doesn't improve in flavour or sweetness. Furthermore, fruit should be fully grown before it can start ripening. Pick it sooner and there isn't much chance of it gladdening either our palates or our hearts.

As in all things, common sense should prevail. Trust your senses when shopping: fruit should look, feel, smell and taste the way nature – at its organic, fully-ripened best – intended. Buy fruit in season and from destinations not too far from where you are. Cold storage and lengthy travelling between farm and kitchen are anathema to perfect fruit.

Treat fruit with the care it deserves. Avoid bruising or piercing it (which invites decay), don't over-chill it (this diminishes the flavour), never leave it languishing in water (who wants soggy fruit?), and watch for that magical moment when it's at full, perfect, eat-me ripeness. Seize it and devour it, as one would seize love, life and opportunity.

Enjoy the pages that follow; have fun cooking with fruit and journeying – as we did – in the sweet company of nature's best. Life may never be the same again.

Laurice

Brunch

'Life is like a grapefruit. It's orange and squishy, and has a few pips in it, and some folks have half a one for breakfast.'

Douglas Adams

Buttermilk Flapjacks with Roasted Pears

Serves 8

Roasted Pears

6 pears

juice of 2 oranges

2 tablespoons clear honey

1 cinnamon stick, crumbled

crème fraîche and extra honey, to serve

Buttermilk Flapjacks

250g cake flour

1 tablespoon baking powder

½ teaspoon salt

3 tablespoons castor sugar

2 tablespoons vegetable oil, plus extra for cooking

2 eggs

125ml buttermilk

250ml milk

Roasted Pears Set the oven at 180°C. Peel, quarter and core the pears and arrange in a baking dish to flg snugly. Pour over the orange juice and honey. Add the cinnamon. Seal the dish with foil and bake for about 45 minutes until the pears are tender (the cooking time will depend on ripeness). Turn the pears in the syrup once or twice while cooking.

Remove the foil, switch on the oven grill and grill the pears for about 10 minutes until the edges are well browned. Transfer to a serving bowl and cool to room temperature.

Buttermilk Flapjacks Sift together the flour, baking power, salt and castor sugar. Lightly mix togothor the oil, eggs, buttermilk and milk, and mix into the dry ingredients to form a smooth batter.

Heat a little oil in a frying pan, drop in large spoonfuls of the batter (you'll need 16 flapjacks) and cook until they are golden and surface bubbles pop. Flip over and cook the other side. Drain on kitchen paper, then arrange on a serving plate.

To Serve Pass around the flapjacks, roasted pears, crème fraîche and honey for guests to help themselves.

Fruit Sticks with Honeyed Yoghurt

Serves 6

Fruit Sticks

425g tin pitted black cherries

565g tin pitted lychees

2 bananas

24 lemon leaves

lemon juice

Honeyed Yoghurt

500ml plain yoghurt

½ teaspoon ground ginger

½ teaspoon ground cardamom

½ teaspoon ground cinnamon

¼ teaspoon grated nutmeg

1 tablespoon clear honey, plus extra for serving

Fruit Sticks Drain the cherries and lychees. Peel the bananas and cut into chunks. Thread the fruit onto bamboo skewers with the lemon leaves and place in a flat dish. Squeeze over a little lemon juice to prevent the bananas from discolouring. Chill in the fridge until serving time; they'll be fine for a couple of hours.

Honeyed Yoghurt Tip the yoghurt into a bowl and mix in the ginger, cardamom, cinnamon, nutmeg and honey. Cover and chill; it will be fine overnight.

To Serve Place the fruit sticks on plates and drizzle over a little honey. Serve honeyed yoghurt in small pots on the side.

Tropical Compôte of Dried Fruit

Serves 6 to 8

500g soft-dried mixed fruit (prunes, peaches, pears, apricots, apples)

500ml fruit nectar (any flavour of your choice)

1 tablespoon brown sugar

1 lemon, thinly sliced

2 cinnamon sticks

6 whole cloves

4 cardamom pods, lightly crushed

2 stalks lemon grass, lightly bruised

plain yoghurt, to serve

Tip the fruit into a medium saucepan and add the fruit nectar, brown sugar, lemon slices, cinnamon, cloves, cardamom and lemon grass. Cover and bring to the boil, then remove from the heat and set aside for a couple of hours for the fruit to plump up nicely.

Transfer the fruit and syrup to a serving bowl and chill in the fridge, where it will remain quite happily for five days.

To Serve Spoon the compôte into bowls and serve with plain yoghurt.

'If you enjoy the fruit, pick not the flower.' Anonymous

Kiwi and Berry Smoothies

It's fun to have layers of contrasting fruit purées, but remember to use the thickest (and heaviest) as a base. Alternatively, swirl them prettily in tall glasses. The best smoothies are well chilled before serving, especially if you're going the 'layering' route.

Serves 2

Smoothies

3 large scoops vanilla ice-cream

375ml plain yoghurt

1 banana, peeled and roughly chopped

½ teaspoon vanilla extract

2 tablespoons clear honey

Fruit Purées

3 kiwi fruit, peeled and chopped

200g raspberries (or other berries of your choice)

castor sugar or clear honey (optional)

Smoothies Whizz all the smoothie ingredients together in a blender or food processor until smooth. Pour into a jug and chill in the fridge.

Fruit Purées Purée the kiwi fruit and berries separately. Check the flavour and add a dash of castor sugar or honey if you feel it's necessary. Chill everything well in separate jugs. Just before serving, whisk again lightly.

To Serve Layer the smoothie and fruit purées in tall glasses and serve pronto.

'Truth is a fruit which should not be plucked until it is ripe.' Voltaire

Sozzled Melons with Roasted Nuts

Serves 6 to 8

Sozzled Melons

½ sweet melon (spanspek)

½ winter melon

1 small pawpaw or papaya

2 slices watermelon

3 tablespoons castor sugar

3 tablespoons tequila

3 tablespoons gin

leaves from a small bunch mint, finely shredded

plain yoghurt, to serve

Roasted Nuts

50g hazelnuts, roughly chopped

3 tablespoons sunflower seeds

3 tablespoons sesame seeds

Sozzled Melons Peel and seed all the fruit and cut into chunks. Combine in a glass bowl, sprinkle with castor sugar and add the tequila, gin and shredded mint. Toss everything together well. Cover and chill for a couple of hours to allow the flavours to infuse.

Roasted Nuts Roast the nuts and seeds in a dry frying pan, tossing them about until they're lightly roasted. Allow to cool.

To Serve Spoon the fruit into bowls, and top with a spoonful of yoghurt and a scattering of roasted nuts and seeds.

Oven-Roasted Tomatoes with Poached Eggs and Bacon

Serves 4

olive oil

8 large roma tomatoes, thickly sliced

sugar, salt, milled black pepper

4 eggs

8 rashers rindless streaky bacon

vegetable oil

hot, buttered toast, to serve

Heat the oven to 180ºC. Line a baking tray with foil and brush (or spray) lightly with olive oil. Lay the tomato slices on top, season with sugar, salt and pepper, and roast for about 30 minutes until semi-dried and intensely flavoured.

To poach the eggs, bring plenty of water to the boil in a wide, shallow saucepan. (Add a tablespoon of vinegar if the eggs aren't fresh from the coop.) Crack in the eggs, cover the pan, and turn the heat to low. It will take about 3 minutes for the eggs to be perfectly cooked. Lift from the water with a slotted spoon and drain well.

While the eggs are poaching, fry the bacon in a dash of oil in a frying pan.

To Serve Arrange roasted tomato on warm plates with the poached eggs and bacon. Serve with hot, buttered toast.

Lemon Curd

Makes about 750ml

6 egg yolks

200g castor sugar

finely grated zest of 4 medium lemons

250ml lemon juice

125g butter, cut into small blocks

Place the egg yolks and castor sugar in a heavy saucepan and whisk off the heat until well blended. Mix in the lemon zest and juice and cook over low heat, stirring constantly, until the mixture thickens like custard. Don't allow it to boil or it may curdle. Remove immediately from the heat.

Whisk the diced butter into the lemon curd, then pour into hot, sterilised jars and allow to cool. Cover with waxed paper and seal. Store in the fridge.

Gingered Quince Preserve

Makes about 1 litre

1kg quinces (4 medium)

salted water

500g sugar

1 litre water

1 teaspoon crushed green ginger

Rub the quinces gently under cold running water to remove all the soft down. Peel, remove the seeds and slice the fruit. Soak in a bowl of salted water for about 30 minutes. Ensure that the fruit is submerged, otherwise it will discolour.

Place the sugar and water in a large saucepan and bring to the boil, stirring constantly until the sugar dissolves. Drain the fruit, add to the pan with the ginger, and simmer very gently, partially covered, until the fruit is soft and the syrup is richly coloured and thick enough to reach setting point. This will take about 1½ to 2 hours.

Pack the fruit in hot sterilised jars and pour in the syrup. Seal and store in a cool cupboard. Serve with toast, or a selection of fresh fruits and a variety of cheeses.

'All happiness depends on a leisurely breakfast.' John Gunther

Tea Time

'It is only the tree loaded with fruit that people throw stones at.'

French Proverb

Apple and Feta Cupcakes

These must be served straight from the oven, but you could keep the batter in the fridge for up to three days.

Makes about 20

250g self-raising flour

pinch salt

100g butter

2 eggs

125ml milk

1 wheel feta cheese, crumbled

12 sweet apples, peeled, cored and cut into small chunks

Grease the cups of a standard muffin tin. Heat the oven to 200°C.

Sift the flour and salt into a bowl, or a food processor. Melt the butter, then lightly beat in the eggs and milk. Add the liquid to the flour and work in without over-mixing (this will make the cupcakes tough.) Mix in the feta and apple chunks.

Place heaped tablespoons of the mixture into the muffin cups and bake for about 15 minutes until the cupcakes are cooked and well browned. Serve warm with butter.

Citrus Whisky Cake

Serves 10 to 12

200ml whisky
200g sultanas
1 lemon
2 eggs
200g castor sugar
250ml milk
100g butter, melted
250g cake flour
1 teaspoon baking powder
1 teaspoon bicarbonate of soda
pinch salt
100g pecan nuts, roughly crumbled
whipped cream, to serve

Syrup

125ml orange juice
4 tablespoons sugar

Grease a 22cm spring-form cake tin. Heat the oven to 170°C. Warm the whisky in a small saucepan, add the sultanas and set aside for about 15 minutes to plump. Drain the sultanas and pop them into a food processor (keep the whisky for the syrup). Cut the lemon into chunks, discard the pips and add to the sultanas. Purée the fruit to a fine paste. Remove from the food processor and set aside.

Place the eggs and castor sugar in the processor and whizz until light and fluffy. Mix in the milk and melted butter. Sift in the flour, baking powder, bicarb and salt and mix in, followed by the lemon paste and pecans. Pour the batter into the cake tin and bake for about 45 minutes until the cake is cooked and a skewer comes out clean.

Syrup Combine the orange juice, sugar and reserved whisky in a small saucepan and heat, stirring until the sugar dissolves. Pour the hot syrup over the cake as it comes out of the oven. Allow to cool before turning out onto a plate.

To Serve Slice the cake and serve with plenty of whipped cream and a lemon wedge for fun.

Choc Almond Torte with Granadilla Coulis

Serves 8 to 10

125ml whisky
50g sultanas
200g dark chocolate, chopped
125g butter
3 eggs, separated
150g castor sugar
120g cake flour
1 teaspoon baking powder
100g nibbed almonds, dry-roasted

Granadilla Coulis
pulp of 6 granadillas
(or 2 x 115g tins)
2 tablespoons castor sugar
2 teaspoons cornflour
6 tablespoons water

Lightly grease a 22cm spring-form cake tin and line the base neatly with baking paper. Set the oven at 170°C. Warm half the whisky, pour over the sultanas and set aside for about 15 minutes to plump.

Melt together the chocolate, butter and remaining whisky in a bowl over simmering water. Stir until smooth, then cool to room temperature. Beat together the egg yolks and castor sugar until thick and pale. Fold in the cooled chocolate mixture and sultanas (with the whisky). Sift in the flour and baking powder, and fold in with the almonds.

Whisk the egg whites stiffly, fold into the batter and pour into the prepared baking tin. Bake for 25 minutes. The outside of the cake will be firm; the centre still slightly moist. Cool the cake in the tin for 10 minutes before unmoulding onto a plate. Peel off the paper.

Granadilla Coulis While the cake is baking, mix together the granadilla pulp and castor sugar in a small saucepan and bring to the boil. Mix together the cornflour and water, stir in, and simmer until the sauce thickens. Allow to cool.

To Serve Slice the cake and spoon granadilla coulis alongside. A mint sprig will tart up the presentation if you're feeling frivolous. To flossy things up even more, sift icing sugar onto both the cake and the plate.

Crunchy Apple, Banana and Nut Cake

Serves 6 to 8

200g brown sugar

120g cake flour, sifted

½ teaspoon baking powder

½ teaspoon bicarbonate of soda

½ teaspoon mixed spice

50g cold butter, cut into blocks

125ml milk

1 egg

2 sweet apples, peeled and thinly sliced

2 bananas, peeled and sliced

100g brazil nuts, roughly chopped and dry-roasted

mascarpone cheese or crème fraîche, to serve

Heat the oven to 180°C. Grease a 22cm cake tin (round or square; non-stick is best). Mix together the brown sugar, flour, baking powder, bicarb and mixed spice. Rub in the butter until the mixture is finely crumbled. Spread half into the cake tin.

Thoroughly mix together the milk and egg, then mix into the remaining flour and butter mixture. Mix in the apples, bananas and half the nuts. Spoon onto the crumb mixture in the tin and bake for about 30 minutes until the cake is cooked and a skewer comes out clean.

Cool the cake in the tin, then lift onto a plate. Slice and serve with a spoonful of mascarpone cheese or crème fraîche. Scatter over the remaining nuts for added crunch.

Warm Apricot Tart

Serves 8

200g cake flour

½ teaspoon baking powder

pinch salt

2 tablespoons castor sugar

125g cold butter, cut into blocks

825g tin apricot halves, well drained

100g sugar

1 teaspoon ground cinnamon

2 egg yolks

250ml plain yoghurt

Set the oven at 200°C. Lightly oil a 25cm loose-based cake tin. Sift together the flour, baking powder, salt and castor sugar. Rub in the butter until the mixture is finely crumbled. Press the mixture into the base and up the sides of the baking tin.

Arrange the fruit in the pastry in neat circles, and sprinkle the sugar and cinnamon on top. Beat together the egg yolks and yoghurt and pour evenly over the fruit. Bake for 35 to 40 minutes until the tart is set and golden. Serve warm or cool.

Gooseberry Cheesecake

If fresh gooseberries aren't in season, use any fresh berries you fancy.

Serves 12

Biscuit Crust

100g brazil nuts

200g crisp biscuits, roughly crushed

80g butter, melted

Filling

250g cream cheese

4 tablespoons castor sugar

3 eggs, separated

finely grated zest and juice of 1 large lemon

1 teaspoon powdered gelatine

125ml cream

100g gooseberries

Biscuit Crust Heat the oven to 180°C. Whizz together the nuts and biscuits in a food processor. Mix in the melted butter, then line a greased 22cm spring-form cake tin. Bake for about 10 minutes until the crust is lightly browned. Allow to cool.

Filling Beat together the cream cheese, castor sugar, egg yolks and lemon zest in a large bowl. Squeeze the lemon juice into a saucepan, warm gently on the stovetop, then remove from the heat. Sprinkle the gelatine onto the surface, allow to sponge, then stir until it dissolves. Mix into the cream cheese mixture.

Whip the egg whites and cream stiffly in separate bowls. Fold into the cream cheese mixture. Pour the filling into the biscuit crust, and chill in the fridge for at least 30 minutes.

To Serve Unmould the cheesecake onto a large platter and pile the gooseberries prettily on top.

'One cannot think well, love well, sleep well, if one has not dined well.' Virginia Woolf

Chocolate Banana Tart

Serves 8 to 10

Pastry

120g cake flour, sifted

pinch salt

4 tablespoons castor sugar

50g cold butter, cut into blocks

1 egg yolk

2 tablespoons iced water (approximate amount)

Chocolate Filling

150g dark chocolate, chopped

100g unsalted butter, cut into blocks

125ml cocoa powder

4 egg yolks

200g castor sugar

4 tablespoons crème fraîche, plus extra for serving

3 tablespoons golden syrup

3 bananas

icing sugar, for dusting

Pastry Mix together the flour, salt and castor sugar. Rub in the butter with your fingertips (or in a food processor) until the mixture is crumbly. Mix in the egg yolk and sufficient iced water to make a soft dough. Wrap in waxed paper and chill in the fridge for a couple of hours to firm up.

Heat the oven to 200°C. Roll out the pastry on a floured board and line a 26cm quiche tin. Line the pastry with lightly oiled foil and bake for 10 minutes. Remove the foil and to bake for 5 to 10 minutes more until pastry is cooked and firm. Allow to cool.

Chocolate Filling Heat the oven to 150°C. Melt the chocolate and butter in a bowl over a pan of simmering water. Remove from the heat. Sift in the cocoa and mix in thoroughly. Whisk together the egg yolks and castor sugar until thick and pale. Mix in the crème fraîche and golden syrup. Fold in the chocolate butter. Pour the filling into the crust and bake for about 40 minutes until set.

Cool the tart on a wire rack, then remove from the baking tin and place on a plate. Slice the bananas and arrange on top. Dust with icing sugar and glaze with a blowtorch or under the oven grill to caramelise the sugar.

To Start

'Ignorance is like a delicate fruit; touch it and the bloom is gone.'

Oscar Wilde

Pear, Gooseberry and Bocconcini Spears with Chilli-Lime Drizzle

Serves 4

2 firm pears

16 gooseberries

16 small bocconcini balls

Chilli-Lime Drizzle

4 tablespoons lemon or lime juice

2 tablespoons sugar

1 red chilli, seeded and finely sliced

Slice the pears into wedges and discard the cores (keep the skin on). Spear onto slim bamboo skewers with the gooseberries and bocconcini balls.

Chilli-Lime Drizzle Combine the lemon or lime juice, sugar and chilli in a small saucepan and heat, stirring until the sugar dissolves. Allow to cool.

To Serve Arrange the skewers on plates and pour over the chilli-lime drizzle.

Green Asparagus with Mixed Berries

Serves 4

200g green asparagus, washed and trimmed

150g blueberries

150g small strawberries

2 tablespoons balsamic vinegar

2 tablespoons macadamia oil

1 teaspoon sugar

Lightly cook the asparagus. Rinse the berries. Reserve a couple of the prettiest for garnishing. Destalk the rest and pop them into a food processor with the balsamic vinegar, macadamia oil and sugar. Whizz until smoothly blended. Check and correct the flavour, adding a little extra sugar if necessary.

To Serve Place asparagus on serving plates with a pool of berry sauce alongside. Pile the reserved berries on top.

Antipasto with Pickled Grapes

Serves 8 to 10

Pickled Grapes

200g green grapes

200g black grapes

2 cinnamon sticks

200ml red wine vinegar

200ml water

200ml brown sugar

5 whole cloves

1 teaspoon black peppercorns

½ teaspoon turmeric

2 teaspoons dry English mustard

Antipasto

sliced meats like parma ham, mortadella, pastrami and baked ham

calamata olives

cubed feta cheese

fresh or tinned artichokes

crusty bread, to serve

Pickled Grapes Sterilise a 1 litre bottle, or two 500ml bottles. Destalk the grapes and remove the pips if necessary, then pack into the jars with the cinnamon sticks.

Place the vinegar, water, brown sugar, cloves, peppercorns, turmeric and mustard in a medium saucepan, and stir over medium heat until the sugar dissolves. Bring to the boil, then reduce the heat and simmer uncovered for 5 minutes. Pour over the fruit to cover it completely. Keep in the fridge for a week before using, if possible, as the flavours get better and better.

Antipasto Arrange everything beautifully on a large platter and pile the pickled grapes into a bowl. Serve with plenty of crusty bread.

'The smallest seed of faith is better than the largest fruit of happiness.'

Henry David Thoreau

Figs and Parma Ham with Sweet Wine Chilli Vinaigrette

Serves 6

6 figs

6 slices parma ham

30g rocket

shaved parmesan cheese

Sweet Wine Chilli Vinaigrette

250ml late harvest wine

½ red chilli, seeded and sliced

juice of 2 limes

4 tablespoons olive oil

salt and milled black pepper

Cut a cross in the base of the figs and squeeze very gently to reveal the insides. Arrange on plates with the parma ham and rocket.

Sweet Wine Chilli Vinaigrette
Pour the wine into a small saucepan, add the chilli and simmer uncovered until reduced to about two tablespoons. Remove from the heat, whisk in the lime juice and olive oil, and season with salt and pepper.

To Serve Drizzle the dressing over the figs, ham and rocket and garnish your creation with parmesan shavings.

Aubergine Crisps and Sliced Quince

Serves 4

Sliced Quince

1 quince

salt

1 small onion, very finely sliced

1 garlic clove, peeled and crushed

1 small red or green chilli, seeded and finely chopped

1 tablespoon fish sauce

2 tablespoons sugar

1 tablespoon lime juice

milled black pepper

Aubergine Crisps

2 medium aubergines

olive oil

Sliced Quince Peel and core the quince, then slice as finely as possible. Sprinkle with salt and set aside for an hour or two. Rinse under cold running water, drain well and dry thoroughly with a clean tea towel. Mix in a bowl with the remaining ingredients, cover and chill.

Aubergine Crisps Slice the aubergine thinly (leave the skin on), and brush each slice well with olive oil on both sides. Heat a non-stick frying pan over high heat and fry the aubergine for a minute or two on each side until golden and crisp.

To Serve Arrange the quince and aubergine on plates. Finish the presentation with a generous drizzle of olive oil, a sprinkling of salt and a twist of the pepper mill.

Seared Scallops with Thai Pawpaw

Thai pawpaw is equally delicious with seared salmon or tuna, or sliced rare-roasted fillet steak.

Serves 4

Seared Scallops

12 scallops

vegetable oil

salt and milled black pepper

Thai Pawpaw

1 medium, under-ripe pawpaw or papaya

2 garlic cloves, peeled and crushed

1 red chilli, seeded and finely sliced

1 tablespoon brown sugar

3 tablespoons lime juice

2 tablespoons fish sauce

2 spring onions, finely sliced

small bunch basil, shredded

small bunch mint, shredded

small bunch coriander, chopped

Seared Scallops Trim off the dark strings of the scallops (the intestinal tract). Rinse thoroughly and pat dry.

Thai Pawpaw Peel and seed the pawpaw, and slice into thin strips. Set aside in a bowl. In another bowl mix together the garlic, chilli, brown sugar, lime juice, fish sauce, spring onions and herbs. Pour over the pawpaw and toss gently to mix.

To Serve Heat a non-stick frying pan over high heat until piping hot. Add a dash of oil and cook the scallops for 2 minutes on one side. Flip over and cook for a minute more. Season lightly with salt and pepper.

Spoon pawpaw onto four plates (or scallop shells if you have them) and top each serving with three scallops and an extra flourish of fresh herbs, if you wish.

Two-Fruit Crostini with Buffalo Mozzarella and Pomegranate

Serves 4

8 slices crusty bread
olive oil
1 peeled garlic clove
1 ball buffalo mozzarella (about 180g), sliced
salt and milled black pepper
1 kiwi fruit, peeled and sliced
1 nectarine or freestone peach, peeled and sliced
1 pomegranate

Brush the bread lightly on both sides with olive oil. Place on a baking tray and toast on both sides under a hot oven grill until crisp and golden. Rub the hot toasts with garlic and place on plates.

Top with sliced mozzarella, season generously with salt and pepper, then add slices of kiwi fruit and nectarines or peaches.

Cut the pomegranate in half, hold over a bowl and gently shake and smack the fruit until the seeds fall out. Scatter them over and around the crostini. Drizzle over a little extra olive oil and serve promptly while the crostini are still warm.

soups

'Wishing to be a friend is quick work, but friendship is a slow-ripening fruit.'

Aristotle

Chilled Gingered Melon Soup

Serves 6

juice of 3 oranges

juice of 2 lemons

2 tablespoons clear honey

6 slices peeled green ginger

1 small sweet melon (spanspek)

Bring the orange juice, lemon juice, honey and ginger to the boil in a small saucepan. Cover and set aside for about 20 minutes for the flavours to infuse.

Peel and seed the melon, cut into chunks and pop them into a food processor. Strain in the orange juice mixture and whizz until the soup is smoothly blended. Chill in the fridge before serving in scooped-out melon shells.

Sherried Tomato Soup

Serves 6

800g very ripe tomatoes

400g tin whole peeled tomatoes

2 leeks, finely sliced

olive oil

1 litre vegetable stock

2 whole cloves

1 bay leaf

1 teaspoon paprika

2 teaspoons sugar

salt and milled black pepper

3 tablespoons medium dry sherry

Blanch the tomatoes in boiling water, then drain well. Peel and chop finely. Chop the tinned tomatoes in their juice and mix in.

Soften the leeks in a little olive oil in a large saucepan. Add the tomato, stock, cloves, bay leaf, paprika and sugar, and season with salt and pepper. Cover and simmer for about 30 minutes until the tomatoes are tender and mushy. Stir in the sherry. Check the flavour and consistency, and adjust if necessary; you might need to add extra sugar if the tomatoes are acidic. Serve hot or chilled.

Cool Avocado Soup with Coriander

Serves 4

2 avocados
3-4 spring onions, trimmed
small bunch coriander
500ml chicken stock
125ml plain yoghurt
salt and milled black pepper

Skin, stone and roughly chop the avocados. Roughly chop the spring onion and pop into a blender or food processor with the coriander. Whizz until finely chopped. Add the avocados, stock and yoghurt and blend until smooth. Season with salt and pepper. Chill the soup in the fridge for up to a day before serving. Some extra coriander sprigs on top will flossy up the presentation no end.

Curried Carrot and Apple Soup

Serves 6

700g carrots, peeled and sliced

2 Granny Smith apples, peeled and chopped

4 leeks, sliced

1,5 litres vegetable stock

½ teaspoon curry powder

½ teaspoon turmeric

sugar, salt, milled black pepper

125ml cream

croûtons, to serve

Toss the carrots, apples and leeks into a large saucepan with a cupful of the stock. Cover and simmer over gentle heat for about 10 minutes. Add the curry powder and turmeric, and season with a little sugar, salt and pepper. Pour in the remaining stock, cover and simmer for about 45 minutes until the vegetables are soft.

Purée the soup smoothly in a food processor or blender, then pour back into the pan. Add the cream and reheat. Check the flavour, and adjust if necessary.

To Serve Serve the soup piping hot with croûtons bobbing about merrily on top.

'Cooking is like love. It should be entered into with abandon or not at all.'
Harriet Van Horne

Salads

'You've got to go out on a limb sometimes because that's where the fruit is.'
Will Rogers

Pawpaw, Pear and Avocado with Blue Cheese Dressing

Serves 4 to 6

1 small pawpaw or papaya

1 pear

1 avocado

lemon juice

30g rocket

Blue Cheese Dressing

2 tablespoons white wine vinegar

4 tablespoons plain yoghurt

200ml vegetable oil

1 teaspoon clear honey

salt and milled black pepper

30g blue cheese, crumbled

Peel, pip and slice the pawpaw, pear and avocado. Squeeze over a little lemon juice to prevent discolouration.

Blue Cheese Dressing Whizz the dressing ingredients together smoothly in a blender or food processor.

To Serve Scatter the rocket on a platter (or smaller plates for individual servings) and top with the fruit. Pour over a little of the dressing, and offer the rest separately.

Caesar Salad with Avocado

Serves 6

Croûtons

6 slices crusty bread

2 garlic cloves, peeled and finely chopped

olive oil

Caesar Dressing

1 egg

2 teaspoons dijon mustard

2 anchovy fillets, drained and finely chopped

1 garlic clove, peeled and finely chopped

juice of 1 small lemon

250ml vegetable oil (or half vegetable, half olive oil)

salt and milled black pepper

Salad

2 cos lettuces

1 avocado

4 anchovy fillets, drained and sliced lengthwise into slim strips

plenty of shaved parmesan cheese

Croûtons Heat the oven to 200°C. Cut the bread into rough chunks and scatter into a roasting pan with the garlic. Drizzle with a little olive oil. Bake for about 15 minutes until the croûtons are toasted and golden brown. Toss them about occasionally so they brown evenly.

Caesar Dressing Prepare in a food processor or in a bowl with a whisk. Whisk together the egg, dijon mustard, anchovies, garlic and lemon juice. With the machine on (or whisking constantly), add the oil in a thin stream. Season with salt and pepper.

To Serve Pile the lettuce leaves into a bowl and pour over half the dressing. Toss well and arrange on a wide platter. Peel and stone the avocado and slice lengthwise into strips. Add to the salad and garnish with anchovy fillets, parmesan shavings and croûtons. Offer the remaining dressing separately for those who may want a little more.

Tossed Rocket with Prosciutto and Watermelon

Serves 2

60g rocket

olive oil

lemon juice

70g prosciutto

1 slice watermelon, peeled, pipped and sliced

1 wheel feta cheese, crumbled

30g blue cheese, crumbled

milled black pepper

Place the rocket into a bowl and moisten with a drizzle of olive oil and a good squeeze of lemon juice. Toss well, then pile onto plates. Garnish with prosciutto, watermelon, feta and blue cheese, and finish off with a generous grind of the pepper mill. If there's no watermelon around, use winter melon instead.

Tomato, Melon and Cannellini Beans with Sesame Dressing

Serves 4 to 5

½ winter melon or sweet melon (spanspek)

2 large tomatoes

400g tin cannellini beans, drained

2-3 leeks, finely sliced

small bunch coriander, roughly chopped

Sesame Dressing

2 tablespoons olive oil

1 tablespoon sesame oil

1 teaspoon soy sauce

juice of 1 lime

salt and milled black pepper

Peel and pip the melon and cut into cubes. Toss into a bowl. Blanch the tomatoes in boiling water, then drain well. Peel away the skins, cut into quarters, and add to the melon. Add the beans, leeks and coriander.

Sesame Dressing Lightly whisk together the dressing ingredients, pour over the salad, and toss gently to mix. Cover and chill for an hour or two, if you wish, for the flavours to merge, but serve the salad at room temperature.

Honeyed Butternut with Prickly Pears and Peanut Splash

Serves 4 to 6

2 prickly pears

1 medium butternut, about 750g

olive oil

1 tablespoon clear honey

pinch ground cinnamon

salt and milled black pepper

Peanut Splash

125ml vegetable oil

1 tablespoon smooth peanut butter

1 tablespoon brown sugar

½ teaspoon dijon mustard

1 tablespoon balsamic vinegar

1 teaspoon sesame oil

Peel the prickly pears and slice thinly. Set aside for later.

Heat the oven to 180°C. Peel and pip the butternut and slice lengthwise into slim strips. Arrange in a single layer in a baking dish to fit snugly. Drizzle over a generous amount of olive oil, then add the honey and sprinkle with cinnamon and a little salt and pepper.

Bake for about 30 minutes until the butternut is tender. Baste with the pan juices, then turn on the oven grill to brown the slices nicely.

Peanut Splash Whisk the ingredients together in a bowl.

To Serve Arrange the butternut and prickly pear artfully on a serving plate. Pour over any remaining pan juices from the butternut. Dress with a little of the peanut splash and offer the rest separately.

Asian Duck and Lychee Salad

Serves 5 to 6

1 free-range pekin duck
3-4 ribs celery, trimmed
2-3 leeks, trimmed
1 orange, quartered
2 teaspoons black peppercorns
6 peeled garlic cloves
4 slices peeled green ginger
750ml water
400g tin pitted lychees
salt and milled black pepper
4 tablespoons ketjap manis (sweet soy sauce)

For the Salad

60g watercress
50g roasted peanuts
1 red onion, finely sliced

Clean the duck. Place the giblets (not the liver; save that for pâté) in a deep saucepan with the celery, leeks, orange, peppercorns, garlic and ginger. Add the water. Drain the lychees and add the syrup to the pan (reserve the fruit).

Cover the pan and bring to the boil. Add the duck and, if the stock doesn't cover it completely, top up with boiling water. Cover and simmer for about 1 hour until the duck is cooked.

Carefully lift the duck from the stock and set it aside to cool. Meanwhile, prepare the stock for the dressing. Spoon off all the fat from the surface (keep it for roasting potatoes). Drain the stock into a clean saucepan; discard the solids.

Boil uncovered until reduced to a light glaze; you will need about a quarter of a cupful. Remove from the heat, season with salt and pepper and stir in the ketjap manis.

Remove and discard all the duck fat, sinews and bones and shred the meat with your fingers. You will have about 400g. Season with a little salt and pepper. Pour over the dressing and toss to mix.

To Serve Scatter the watercress onto a platter and top with the dressed duck. Garnish with peanuts, onion slices and lychees. To retain the Asian mood, eat with chopsticks.

Créole Tomatoes and Plums with Spiked Basil Drizzle

Serves 4 to 6

Spiked Basil Drizzle

125ml olive oil

juice of ½ lemon

few drops Tabasco pepper sauce

salt and milled black pepper

2 tablespoons shredded basil leaves

Créole Tomatoes and Plums

300g roma or rosa tomatoes

2 plums

1 purple onion, peeled and sliced

1 wheel feta cheese, roughly crumbled

Spiked Basil Drizzle Whisk the ingredients together.

Créole Tomatoes and Plums Cut the tomatoes in half or quarters and toss them into a bowl. Stone the plums, slice thickly and add to the tomatoes with the onion and feta. Pour over the spiked basil drizzle, toss everything together, then pile onto plates.

To Serve Garnish the salad with small, tender basil leaves, if you have a few handy.

Mains

‘Although one may fail to find happiness in theatrical life, one never wishes to give it up after having once tasted its fruits.’

Anna Pavlova

Fishcakes on Apricot-Flecked Lentils

If you can't find trout, any sort of fish will do, leftover or freshly cooked.

Serves 4 to 6

Apricot-Flecked Lentils

1 red onion, finely sliced

olive oil

2 teaspoons roasted masala (page 111) or curry powder

400g tin brown lentils, drained

200g soft-dried apricots, chopped

salt and milled black pepper

1 tablespoon balsamic vinegar

2 tablespoons chopped mint leaves

Fishcakes

500g smoked trout fillets

300g potatoes, peeled and diced

4 tablespoons finely chopped onion

3 tablespoons chopped flat-leaf parsley

1 teaspoon turmeric

2 eggs, lightly beaten

juice of 1 lemon or lime

vegetable oil

lemon wedges, for squeezing

Apricot-Flecked Lentils Gently fry the onion in olive oil in a large saucepan until golden. Stir in the masala or curry powder, then add the lentils and apricots and heat through. Season with salt and pepper.

Remove from the heat and stir in the balsamic vinegar and mint. Set aside for an hour or two (overnight is even better) before serving, to allow the flavours to infuse.

Fishcakes Skin and flake the trout, jettisoning all the bones. Place in a large bowl and season generously with salt and pepper.

Cook the potato in salted boiling water. Drain well. Mash and season with salt and pepper. Mix in the fish, onion, parsley, turmeric and egg, and flavour with lemon or lime juice. Form into patties, and flatten slightly between your palms.

To Serve Fry the fishcakes in hot oil until crisp and well browned. Drain on paper towel. Serve on apricot-flecked lentils with lemon wedges for squeezing.

Grilled Fish with Avocado, Melon and Tomato Relish

Serves 4

Grilled Fish

4 fillets fresh fish (skin on), about 200g each

salt and milled black pepper

4 tablespoons olive oil

juice of 1 lemon or lime

Avocado, Melon and Tomato Relish

1 avocado, peeled, stoned and cut into small cubes

½ sweet melon (spanspek), skinned, pipped and cut into small cubes

200g cocktail tomatoes, quartered

small bunch coriander, chopped

3 tablespoons drained capers

3 tablespoons olive oil

juice of 2 limes or 1 large lemon

Grilled Fish Place the fish fillets in a dish to fit snugly, and season with salt and pepper. Pour over the olive oil and lemon or lime juice. Set aside.

Avocado, Melon and Tomato Relish Mix the avocado, melon, tomatoes, coriander and capers in a bowl. Pour over the olive oil and flavour the relish with lime or lemon juice, salt and pepper. Toss everything together.

Just before serving, heat a ridged grill pan on the stovetop and grill the fish flesh-down until well browned. Then turn and grill skin-down until done. Take care you don't overcook the fish and dry it out. Test by parting the flesh with two forks and taking a peek; it should be opaque right through.

To Serve Place the fish on warm plates and spoon a little relish on top or alongside.

'There is no sincerer love than the love of food.' George Bernard Shaw

Island-Style Fish Kebabs with Grapefruit Pickle

Serves 6

1,2 kg filleted fish

salt and milled black pepper

Marinade

200ml olive oil

1 bunch spring onions, finely chopped

juice of 1 lemon

8-10 garlic cloves, peeled and finely chopped

3-4 slices peeled green ginger, finely chopped

2 tablespoons finely chopped lemon grass

leaves pulled from a small bunch thyme

Grapefruit Pickle

2 ruby grapefruit

2 tablespoons olive oil

1 tablespoon yellow mustard seeds

1 small red or green chilli, seeded and finely sliced (optional)

1 tablespoon sugar

4 tablespoons white wine vinegar

Cut the fish into large cubes; remove the skin. Season lightly with salt and pepper.

Marinade Combine the ingredients in a flat dish. Pile in the fish cubes and turn until well coated. Cover and chill for 3 to 4 hours (longer if you prefer a stronger flavour).

Grapefruit Pickle Skin the grapefruit and cut out the segments. Do this over a bowl to collect the juice, and squeeze out the excess with your hands.

Heat the olive oil in a small frying pan and fry the mustard seeds and chilli until the seeds start to pop. Remove from the heat, stir in the sugar, then the vinegar and grapefruit juice. Boil gently uncovered until the syrup thickens. Remove from the heat, add the grapefruit segments and leave to cool.

Thread the fish onto sturdy lemon grass stalks or skewers and grill under a preheated oven grill, or braai over hot coals until well browned and cooked through (about 2 minutes on each side should do it). Brush occasionally with the marinade to keep the fish moist.

To Serve Arrange the kebabs on pretty plates with the grapefruit pickle and a simple salad.

Charred Tuna with West-African Banana Chutney

Serves 4

Banana Chutney

125ml brown sugar

250ml white wine vinegar

1 chilli, sliced (discard the seeds for a milder chutney)

2 cardamom pods, crushed

½ teaspoon cumin seeds

1 bay leaf

4 nearly ripe bananas, peeled and sliced

Charred Tuna

4 tuna steaks, about 100g each

olive oil

salt and milled black pepper

Banana Chutney Combine the brown sugar, vinegar, chilli, cardamom, cumin and bay leaf in a medium saucepan. Heat slowly, stirring until the sugar dissolves. Cover and simmer for about 3 minutes for the flavours to infuse. Add the banana and simmer uncovered just until the fruit is soft and the syrup has thickened. Cooking time depends on the ripeness of the bananas; anything from 1 to 3 minutes should do it.

Charred Tuna Brush the tuna generously with olive oil and season with salt and pepper. Heat a ridged grill pan or heavy frying pan, add the tuna and char well on both sides. Don't cook it all the way through; the fish should be still rare in the centre. Alternatively, braai the fish over medium-hot coals.

To Serve Place the tuna steaks on warm plates or boards with a little banana chutney spooned on top.

Seared Salmon with Potato, Bean and Citrus Salad

Serves 4

Mustard Dressing

125ml olive oil

2 tablespoons lemon or lime juice

1 teaspoon wholegrain mustard

1 teaspoon clear honey

salt and milled black pepper

Potato, Bean and Citrus Salad

12 new potatoes

150g slim green beans

olive oil

1 red onion, finely sliced

4 anchovy fillets, finely sliced

1 grapefruit, peeled and segmented

1 orange, peeled and segmented

small bunch flat-leaf parsley, chopped

Seared Salmon

4 thick salmon fillets, about 100g each

olive oil

lemon juice

Mustard Dressing Whisk the ingredients together.

Potato, Bean and Citrus Salad Boil the potatoes in their jackets until soft. Cut in half or quarters, depending on size. Blanch the beans in salted boiling water until tender but not too floppy, then refresh in cold water. Drain well.

Heat a generous amount of olive oil in a medium frying pan and fry the onion until translucent. Add the anchovies and potatoes, and fry until golden. Add the beans and grapefruit and orange segments, and heat through. Season with salt and pepper. Remove from the heat, add the parsley, pour over the mustard dressing, and mix everything together really well.

Seared Salmon Check the salmon and pull out any bones with a pin boner or tweezers. Season with salt and pepper.

Heat a little olive oil in a non-stick frying pan and fry the fish over high heat for 2 to 3 minutes on each side until lightly caramelised and still slightly pink in the centre. Season with a good squeeze of lemon juice.

To Serve Spoon the potato, bean and citrus salad onto plates and top with slices of salmon. Serve warm or at room temperature, in the Mediterranean way.

Chilli-Garlic Prawns with Mango and Torn Basil

Serves 2 as a main course; 4 as a starter

10-12 large prawns

100g dried egg noodles or rice noodles

olive oil

4 garlic cloves, peeled and crushed

1 red chilli, seeded and finely sliced

lemon juice

salt and milled black pepper

1 mango, peeled, stoned and cut into chunks

small bunch basil, torn into pieces

Remove the prawn heads, shells and veins; leave the tail shells on so they look good.

Pour boiling water over the noodles in a bowl and set aside for about 2 minutes to soften. Drain well in a colander.

Heat a generous splash of olive oil in a frying pan until sizzling hot. Stir in the garlic and chilli, then add the prawns and fry for about 20 seconds on each side. Add a good squeeze of lemon juice, season with salt and pepper, and cook the prawns over very low heat for about 2 minutes until done, depending on size. Don't overcook them!

Add the drained noodles to the pan and toss everything together to heat through. Toss in the mango and basil. Serve immediately, or the charm of the dish will be lost.

Lemon Chicken with Button Mushrooms

Serves 4 to 5

8 free-range chicken thighs, skinned
olive oil and butter
salt and milled black pepper
125ml warm chicken stock
3 lemons, peeled and segmented
6 garlic cloves, peeled and chopped
2 rosemary sprigs, snipped into pieces
2 tablespoons snipped fennel leaves
250g small button mushrooms
lemon slices, for squeezing

Trim the chicken of all excess fat. Heat a little olive oil and butter in a large saucepan with a well-fitting lid. The chicken pieces should fit snugly without overlapping. Lightly brown the chicken on all sides over medium-high heat; watch carefully and turn the pieces frequently so they don't stick to the pan. Season with salt and pepper.

Add the stock, lemon segments, garlic, rosemary and fennel to the pan. Cover and cook over very low heat for about 40 minutes until the chicken is cooked.

Lift the chicken onto a warm platter, cover and keep warm. Add the mushrooms to the pan and cook uncovered over very high heat, stirring occasionally, until they are tender and the liquid has reduced and thickened nicely. Pour the mushrooms and sauce over the chicken and garnish with lemon.

Chicken with Peaches and Pancetta

Mangoes and nectarines are also delicious in this recipe if peaches aren't about.

Serves 4

8 free-range chicken thighs, skinned and boned

8 slices pancetta

butter

1 lime, thinly sliced

1 clingstone peach, peeled, stoned and sliced

leaves pulled from a small bunch thyme

salt and milled black pepper

Heat the oven to 180°C. Wrap each chicken thigh in a slice of pancetta. Generously butter a baking dish large enough to accommodate all the ingredients. Add the lime slices and top with the pancetta-wrapped chicken. Scatter the peach slices and thyme all about and season lightly with salt and pepper.

Bake uncovered for about 35 minutes until the chicken is cooked, the pancetta crisp and the peaches gloriously tender and golden. Serve with no fuss at all, directly from the baking dish.

'Let us learn to appreciate when there will be times when the trees will be bare,
and look forward to the time when we may pick the fruit.'

Anton Chekhov

Chicken and Apricot Sosaties

These delish morsels are best braaied, but there's no law against grilling them under a very hot oven grill. Like most spicings, masalas are available ready-made, but home-made masalas are much fresher and more piquantly spiced. Ours makes 200g, so you'll have lots left over to use in your favourite curry.

Serves 4

Roasted Masala

75g coriander seeds
75g cumin seeds
25g dried red chillies
10g black peppercorns
1 cinnamon stick, broken into small pieces
2g whole cloves
2 teaspoons cardamom pods, crushed
2 teaspoons turmeric
1 teaspoon ground ginger

Chicken and Apricot Sosaties

14 free-range chicken thigh fillets (boneless and skinless)
3 red or yellow peppers, cored and cut into chunks
250g soft-dried apricots
28 lemon leaves
olive oil
salt

Roasted Masala Place the coriander, cumin, chillies, peppercorns, cinnamon, cloves and cardamom in a dry frying pan and roast, tossing lightly until the mixture is aromatic. Remove from the heat and mix in the turmeric and ginger. Allow to cool, then grind fairly finely in a pestle and mortar. Store in a screw-topped jar in a cool cupboard, or in the fridge or freezer.

Chicken and Apricot Sosaties Thread the chicken, peppers, apricots and lemon leaves onto skewers (soak them for a while in warm water if they're made of wood). Lay side-by-side in a roaster, sprinkle liberally with olive oil and sprinkle generously with roasted masala. Turn them over and oil and spice the other side as well. Season lightly with salt.

To Serve Braai the sosaties over hot coals or grill under a preheated oven grill until cooked through and delectably charred. Serve on couscous with your favourite sauce, if you wish; store-bought pesto or chermoula are good.

Pineapple Chicken

Serves 4

4 filleted, skinless free-range chicken breasts, sliced (about 400g)
salt, vegetable oil
1 onion, sliced into slim crescents
3 garlic cloves, peeled and crushed
small knob green ginger, peeled and crushed
½ pineapple, peeled and sliced into chunks
230g tin water chestnuts, drained and sliced
300g small spinach leaves

Sauce

250ml orange juice
3 tablespoons soy sauce
1 tablespoon brown sugar
1 tablespoon white wine vinegar
1 teaspoon oyster sauce
2 teaspoons cornflour

Salt the chicken lightly. Heat a little oil in a wok or large frying pan and stir-fry the onion, garlic and ginger for about 1 minute. Add the pineapple and stir-fry for 1 to 2 minutes. Add the chicken and stir-fry until it is sealed all over.

Sauce Mix together the sauce ingredients and add to the pan, stirring until it becomes clear and thickened. Reduce the heat and cook for 3 to 4 minutes more until the chicken is cooked. Just before serving, add the water chestnuts and spinach and heat through. Serve with noodles or rice.

Moroccan Chicken with Dates

Serves 4 to 5

8 free-range chicken thighs

salt and milled black pepper

200g dried or soft-dried dates

olive oil

1 small onion, finely chopped

4 garlic cloves, peeled and crushed

½ teaspoon ground cumin

¼ teaspoon ground coriander

250ml plain yoghurt

125ml dry white wine

125ml roughly chopped mint

Set the oven at 180°C. Trim the chicken of excess fat (leave the bone in and skin on) and season with salt and pepper. Stone the dates.

Heat a little olive oil in a frying pan, add the onion and garlic and cook until golden and translucent. Add the cumin, coriander, yoghurt, wine and half the mint (reserve the rest for garnishing), and heat through. Season with salt and pepper. Pour into a casserole and nestle in the chicken and dates.

Cover and bake for 30 minutes. Uncover and bake for a further 15 to 20 minutes until the chicken is cooked through and the skin is nicely browned. Garnish with the reserved chopped mint.

'Sleep 'til you're hungry, eat 'til you're sleepy.' Author Unknown

Roasted Chicken with Apple and Garlic

Serves 4

4 free-range chicken breasts on the bone

olive oil

2 red onions, sliced into thick wedges

1 head garlic

5-6 rosemary sprigs, roughly chopped

2 Granny Smith apples, quartered and cored

salt and milled black pepper

brown sugar

125ml apple juice

2 tablespoons apple cider vinegar

4 tablespoons crème fraîche

Heat the oven to 220°C. Trim the chicken breasts of excess fat; leave the bone in and skin on.

Drizzle olive oil into a roaster that will accommodate all the ingredients. Scatter in the onions. Slice the top off the garlic to expose the cloves, break them apart and scatter onto the onion with the rosemary. Place the chicken on top with the apples around. Season the meat with salt and pepper, and the apples with brown sugar.

Roast uncovered for about 50 minutes until the chicken is done, the skin is crisp as can be, and the apples are tinged with brown.

Lift the meat, apples and onions onto a warm platter. Place the roaster on the stovetop, add the apple juice and cider vinegar and boil uncovered until reduced by two-thirds and nicely thickened. Stir in the crème fraîche and heat through. Pour the sauce into a jug and serve separately.

Herb-Roasted Orange and Lemon Chicken with Gremolata Potatoes

Serves 4 to 5

1 whole free-range chicken

salt and milled black pepper

1 orange, quartered

1 lemon, quartered

1 large bunch herbs (parsley, thyme, sage, rosemary)

olive oil

6 potatoes, washed (skins on)

finely grated zest of 1 lemon

small bunch flat-leaf parsley, chopped

6 garlic cloves, peeled and finely chopped

Wash the chicken and pat dry. Season the cavity with salt and pepper, then stuff in the oranges, lemons and herbs. Place in a roasting tray, rub all over with olive oil and season with a little more salt and pepper. Heat the oven to 200°C.

Cut the potatoes into large wedges, toss into a bowl and drizzle with olive oil. Mix in the lemon zest, parsley and garlic, and season with salt and pepper.

Scatter the potatoes around the chicken and roast for about 1¼ hours until the potatoes are wonderfully tender and the chicken is crisp and cooked through (the thigh juices will run clear and the legs will wriggle easily).

To Serve Lift the chicken onto a large platter and arrange the potatoes all about. Pour over the pan juices and serve with a simple salad or lightly-cooked vegetables.

'A man is not an orange. You can't eat the fruit and throw away the peel.'

Arthur Miller

Sausages on Garlic Mash with Mango Chutney

Serves 4

Mango Chutney

2 mangoes

4 spring onions, finely sliced

1-2 red chillies, seeded and sliced (optional)

small bunch basil leaves, roughly torn

2 teaspoons sesame oil

2 tablespoons grape seed oil or olive oil

1 tablespoon balsamic vinegar

salt and milled black pepper

Garlic Mash

4 large potatoes, peeled and diced

5-6 garlic cloves, peeled

olive oil

4 tablespoons chopped parsley

4 tablespoons chopped chives

Sausages

8 sausages (choose your favourite: pork, chicken, beef, boerewors)

vegetable oil

Mango Chutney Peel and stone the mangoes and cut into small chunks. Add the remaining ingredients and mix together. Cover and chill.

Garlic Mash Cook the potatoes and garlic in salted boiling water until soft. Drain off most of the liquid, season with a little salt and pepper, and mash the potatoes with a glug of olive oil until nice and creamy. Mix in the parsley and chives.

Sausages Fry the sausages in a little oil until golden and cooked through, or braai over medium-hot coals if you prefer.

To Serve Spoon garlic mash onto warm plates and top with a couple of sausages. Complete the dish with a little mango chutney on the side.

Pork Medallions with Rooibos-Plumped Prunes

Serves 4

Rooibos-Plumped Prunes

125g soft-dried prunes

1 rooibos teabag

few strips orange peel

juice of 1 orange

5 bay leaves, lightly crushed

4 whole cloves

1 cinnamon stick

1 teaspoon clear honey

Pork Medallions

2-3 plump pork fillets (about 800g)

salt and milled black pepper

butter and olive oil

small bunch sage leaves, shredded

125ml dry white wine

125ml chicken stock

Rooibos-Plumped Prunes Place the prunes in a small saucepan with the remaining ingredients and add sufficient cold water to just cover the fruit. Cover with the lid and simmer for about 10 minutes until the fruit is plump. Uncover and simmer more briskly until the syrup has reduced by half. Discard the teabag and whole spices, and set the prunes aside to cool.

Pork Medallions Trim the pork and season with salt and pepper. Slice the fillets diagonally into thick slices, making them as even as possible. Flatten by whacking with the flat side of a large knife, and season with a little salt and pepper.

Heat a knob of butter and a little oil in a large frying pan until it starts to sizzle and brown. Add the meat and brown well, then turn the slices, rubbing them into the pan to gain colour. Cover and cook over very low heat for about 12 minutes. Transfer the meat to a warm plate and tent with foil to keep warm.

Add the sage, wine and stock to the pan and simmer until the sauce thickens nicely, scraping up all the browning to make it rich and tasty. Check and correct the seasoning.

To Serve Pour the sauce over the meat, top with prunes and serve promptly.

Gammon Steaks with Buttered Vodka Pineapple

Serves 4

4 gammon steaks

olive oil

milled black pepper

1 pineapple

2 tablespoons butter

2 tablespoons vodka

1 tablespoon caramel sugar

Drizzle the gammon steaks with olive oil and season generously with pepper. Heat the oven to 200ºC. Cut the skin off the pineapple and cut into wedges through the leafy top so that it looks glamorous. Arrange in a small baking tray, dot with butter, pour over the vodka and sprinkle with caramel sugar. Place in the oven, switch on the grill and grill for about 35 minutes, turning the fruit regularly and basting with the pan juices so that it cooks evenly. When the pineapple is tender and golden, it's ready.

To Serve Heat a ridged grill pan until piping hot and grill the gammon for 2 to 3 minutes on each side. Place on warm plates with pineapple alongside. Mashed potato is a great accompaniment.

Roast Pork with Herbed Apples

Serves 8

Roast Pork

1,8kg pork roast

wine vinegar

olive oil

salt, cake flour

Herbed Apples

8 Granny Smith apples

8 small bunches of herbs (sage leaves, rosemary, lavender)

1 lime, finely sliced

1 tablespoon brown sugar

6 tablespoons medium dry sherry

4 tablespoons apple jelly

Roast Pork Score the pork skin with a sharp knife. Pour boiling water over, then drain well. Place the meat in a roaster and – if you have time – refrigerate overnight uncovered to dry out the skin.

Heat the oven to 220°C. Sprinkle a little vinegar and olive oil onto the pork and massage in well all over. Season liberally with salt. Roast uncovered for 30 minutes. Reduce the oven temperature to 160°C and continue to roast, calculating 25 minutes per 500g.

To crisp the crackling, sprinkle it lightly with flour and increase the oven temperature to 200°C for another 25 minutes; switch on the oven grill at the end.

Herbed Apples Remove the apple cores and slice into the skins round the circumference. Place in a baking dish to fit snugly. Press the bunches of herbs into the hollows with a slice of lime. Sprinkle a little brown sugar on top.

Pour the sherry round the apples, add the apple jelly and remaining lemon slices and bake uncovered for the final 20 minutes of the pork roast.

To Serve Slice the pork and serve with herbed apples on the side. Spoon over the pan juices from the herbed apples to finish things off nicely. A flourish of extra fresh herbs won't go amiss either!

Chilli Pork Chops with Seared Nectarines

Serves 4

4 plump pork chops

2 nectarines

butter and vegetable oil

4 tablespoons whisky

salt and milled black pepper

1 onion, sliced into crescents

small bunch sage, chopped

1 small red chilli, sliced and seeded

1 cinnamon stick

4 whole cloves

125ml chicken stock

4 tablespoons medium dry sherry

1 tablespoon brown sugar

extra sage leaves, for garnishing

Trim the meat of excess fat. Peel and stone the nectarines, and slice thickly. Heat a little butter and oil in a wide frying pan and lightly brown the nectarines; don't let them get too mushy. Remove from the pan and keep warm.

Add a little extra butter and oil to the pan and fry the pork chops until well browned. Reduce the heat and continue to cook until done right through, turning them from time to time. Pour over the whisky and flame. When the flames die down, remove the meat from the pan and season with salt and pepper. Keep warm.

Add the onion to the pan (with a little more butter if necessary) and cook until softened. Stir in the chopped sage, chilli, cinnamon, cloves, stock, sherry and brown sugar. Boil the sauce uncovered until slightly reduced and thickened.

To Serve Spoon the onion mixture onto warm plates, top with pork chops and garnish with seared nectarines and sage leaves.

Ostrich Steaks with Orange, Onion and Olive Salsa

Serves 4

8 ostrich steaks, about 100g each

olive oil

roasted masala (page 111)

salt and milled black pepper

Herbed Orange, Onion and Olive Salsa

4 oranges

2 tablespoons red wine vinegar or cider vinegar

4 tablespoons olive oil

2 sprigs oregano, chopped

1 red onion, sliced

125ml pitted calamata olives

Place the ostrich steaks in a dish, drizzle generously with olive oil and season with roasted masala, salt and pepper, pressing it firmly into the surface of the meat.

Herbed Orange, Onion and Olive Salsa Peel the oranges, cut in half and slice into a bowl. Whisk together the vinegar, olive oil and oregano, pour over the orange slices and mix in gently. Chill for about 30 minutes in the fridge, then stir in onion and olives, and season with pepper.

Shortly before serving, heat a ridged grill pan until it's searing hot, and grill the ostrich steaks for about 2 minutes on each side until well browned but still pink in the centre. Alternatively, braai the steaks over medium-hot coals.

To Serve Arrange the steaks on warm plates, season with salt and pepper, and spoon the salsa alongside.

Panned Fillet Steaks with Brandied Figs and Peppercorn Sauce

Ask your butcher to cut thick steaks from the middle section of the fillet.

Serves 4

250g soft-dried figs
250ml brandy
4 beef steaks, about 150g each
salt and milled black pepper
butter and olive oil
250ml cream
1 tablespoon green peppercorns, lightly crushed
1 teaspoon dijon mustard
finely grated zest of ½ lemon

Place the figs in a bowl. Warm the brandy, pour over and set aside to soak and plump for a couple of hours.

Season the steaks with salt and pepper. Heat a little butter and oil in a heavy frying pan and brown the meat well on both sides. Cook until done to the desired degree, then place on warm plates.

Drain the figs and pour the brandy into the frying pan with the cream. Boil uncovered until reduced by half and nicely thickened. Stir in the green peppercorns, mustard and lemon zest, check the seasoning and add a little salt and pepper if necessary.

To Serve Pour the sauce over the meat and garnish with figs. Serve with crisp chips and a simple salad.

Rare Roast Fillet with Pear, Aubergine and Tomato Pickle

Serves 6 to 8

Pear, Aubergine and Tomato Pickle

1 medium aubergine (about 300g)

salt and milled black pepper

olive oil

2 onions, roughly sliced

2 firm pears, peeled, cored and cut into chunks

2 large tomatoes, skinned and roughly chopped

1 green chilli, seeded and finely sliced

6-8 garlic cloves, peeled and crushed

small knob green ginger, peeled and crushed

1 teaspoon brown sugar

2 tablespoons white wine vinegar

Rare Roast Fillet

1,5kg whole beef fillet

vegetable oil

Pear, Aubergine and Tomato Pickle Slice the aubergine (leave the skin on), then cut the slices into quarters. Sprinkle with salt, then pile into a colander and set aside for about 20 minutes to dégorge. Rinse with cold water and pat dry with kitchen paper.

Heat a generous amount of olive oil in a wide saucepan with a well-fitting lid and fry the onions until golden. Add the aubergine and fry until lightly sealed. Add the pears and tomatoes, then the chilli, garlic, ginger, brown sugar and vinegar. Season with salt and pepper. Cover and cook over very low heat for 5 minutes.

Rare Roast Fillet Heat the oven to 200°C. Trim the meat, rub all over with olive oil and season with plenty of pepper. Heat a little vegetable oil in a frying pan and brown the meat well all over. Transfer it to a lightly oiled roasting tray and roast for 15 minutes.

Reduce the heat to 180°C and roast for a further 25 to 30 minutes for rare to medium-rare meat with an internal temperature of 60°C on a meat thermometer.

To braai the fillet, prepare a good bed of hot coals. Brown the fillet well all over, then raise the grid from the heat and cook at a more moderate rate. It will be medium-rare in about 40 minutes.

Lift the fillet onto a plate and allow to rest for about 10 minutes.

To Serve Present this dish on a large platter for everyone to help themselves: slice the fillet and spoon the pickle on the side.

Peppercrust Fillet Carpaccio with Avocado and Coriander Mash

Serves 8 to 10

1,5kg whole fillet of beef

salt and crushed black pepper

vegetable oil

6 tablespoons olive oil

4 tablespoons red wine vinegar

4 tablespoons balsamic vinegar

4 tablespoons capers

thyme sprigs, for garnishing

Avocado and Coriander Mash

1 avocado

juice of ½ lemon

small bunch coriander, roughly chopped

Trim the steak, season with a little salt and plenty of crushed pepper. Sear on all sides in hot oil in a heavy pan. Cover the pan, reduce the heat and pan-roast slowly for about 5 minutes. Remove the meat from the pan and allow to cool. Slice thinly and arrange on a serving platter.

Mix together the olive oil and vinegars and drizzle over the meat. Scatter capers and thyme on top.

Avocado and Coriander Mash Skin and stone the avocado, mash roughly and mix in the lemon juice and coriander. Season with salt and pepper.

To Serve The fillet is best served at room temperature, with avocado and coriander mash on the side.

Lamb and Peach Tagine with Chickpeas and Roasted Almonds

Tagines are Moroccan slow-cooked meat, fruit and vegetable dishes which are almost invariably made with lamb.

Serves 4

1kg lean lamb (leg or shoulder)

olive oil

salt and milled black pepper

2 onions, thickly sliced

2 teaspoons ground cumin

1 teaspoon ground coriander

½ teaspoon ground ginger

½ teaspoon ground cinnamon

400g tin whole peeled tomatoes, chopped in their juice

1 red chilli, seeded and finely sliced

250ml beef stock

4 clingstone peaches (or 150g soft-dried peaches)

400g tin chickpeas, drained

small bunch mint, chopped

small bunch coriander, chopped

100g slivered almonds, dry-roasted

Heat the oven to 160°C. Trim the meat of excess fat, and cut into large chunks. Heat a little olive oil in a large saucepan and seal the meat a few pieces at a time. Remove from the pan and season with salt and pepper.

Add the onions to the pan (with a little more oil if necessary) and fry until well browned. Return the meat to the pan, sprinkle over the cumin, coriander, ginger and cinnamon, and stir in. Add the tomatoes, chilli and stock.

Tip everything into a tagine (or a suitable baking dish), cover and bake until the meat is so tender it falls from the bones. This should take 1½ to 2 hours, depending on the cut.

Peel, stone and slice the peaches and add to the tagine with the chickpeas, mint and coriander, and bake for about 5 minutes more until the fruit is soft and the chickpeas are hot. Garnish the tagine with roasted almonds and serve with couscous.

Lamb Chops with Marmalade Plums on Butter Bean Mash

Serves 2

Butter Bean Mash

400g tin butter beans or cannellini beans

4 garlic cloves, peeled

2 tablespoons olive oil

salt and milled black pepper

½ teaspoon ground cumin

pinch smoked Spanish paprika

juice of ½ lemon

small bunch chives, finely chopped

Lamb Chops

4 lamb loin chops, trimmed of excess fat

butter and olive oil

Marmalade Plums

2 plums, quartered and stoned

2 tablespoons brown sugar

1 tablespoon marmalade

4 tablespoons verjuice or dry white wine

2 teaspoons wholegrain mustard

Butter Bean Mash Drain the beans, tip into a food processor and whizz with the garlic and olive oil until well mixed. Season with salt and pepper, then mix in the cumin, paprika, lemon juice and chives.

Lamb Chops Pin the chops with thin metal skewers to keep them nice and neat. Season with salt and pepper. Heat a little butter and olive oil in a heavy frying pan until sizzling hot. Fry the chops, turning often, until done; this should only take 5 to 6 minutes depending on thickness, as they should still be slightly pink inside. Set aside and keep warm.

Marmalade Plums Toss the plums into the pan until lightly glazed. Sprinkle over the brown sugar, then add the marmalade, verjuice or wine and mustard, and cook until the plums are soft and the sauce is thickened and well reduced. Check the seasoning and add salt and pepper to taste.

To Serve Spoon butter bean mash onto warm plates, top with the chops and spoon plums and sauce around.

Afterwards

'A gourmet who thinks of calories is like a tart who looks at her watch.'

James Beard

Strawberries with Yoghurt and Nuts

Serves 4

400g strawberries
castor sugar
4 tablespoons gin or vodka
500g plain yoghurt
100g hazelnuts, roughly chopped

Rinse, drain and hull the strawberries, then slice thickly into a bowl.

Sprinkle over a liitle castor sugar and gin or vodka. Cover and set aside for about an hour in a cool spot to mascerate.

To Serve Spoon the strawberries onto plates, pour over the juice, and top with yoghurt and a scattering of nuts.

Spiced Berry Jellies

Serves 4 to 5

400g berries (raspberries or youngberries are best)
500ml cranberry juice
4 tablespoons sugar
2 whole cloves
2 cinnamon sticks
5 gelatine leaves
125ml port
1 tablespoon lemon juice

Rinse the berries with cold water. Drain well. Pile into glasses (tall; short; martini; champagne – you choose!) and place in the fridge while making the jelly.

Heat the cranberry juice in a medium saucepan with the sugar, cloves and cinnamon, stirring until the sugar dissolves. Don't allow it to boil. Cover and set aside for about 15 minutes for the flavours of the spices to infuse.

Meanwhile, soak the gelatine leaves in a basin of cold water – 5 minutes should be sufficient. Lift from the water and squeeze in your hands to get rid of as much moisture as possible. Add the gelatine to the warm juice and stir until it dissolves. Stir in the port and lemon juice.

Strain the jelly into a jug, then pour it onto the berries in the glasses. Return them to the fridge to set; about 4 to 5 hours will do it.

Honey-Baked Plums with Gorgonzola

Fruit and cheese are happy together, and make a very appealing after-dinner treat. If you're not crazy about blue cheese, use any other cheese you prefer; brie, camembert or duetto (a mixture of blue and cream cheese) are all delicious. Choose plums for baking that are not overripe.

Serves 6

6 plums

4 tablespoons clear honey

2 tablespoons sugar

2 tablespoons apricot or cassis liqueur (optional)

200g gorgonzola or blue cheese

crisp sweet biscuits, to serve

Heat the oven to 180°C. Wash the plums, wipe dry, place stem-side down on a board and cut a cross in the top of each one. As they cook, the skin bursts, revealing the beautiful colour of the flesh.

Place the plums in a baking dish to fit snugly. Drizzle with honey, sprinkle with sugar and pour over the liqueur. Bake uncovered for 20 to 25 minutes until they are soft but not collapsing in a mush. Baste with the syrup from time to time. Cool the plums to room temperature.

To Serve Place chunks or wedges of cheese onto plates with the plums and a little of the syrup. Serve with crisp, sweet biscuits.

'Patience is bitter, but it bears sweet fruit.' Turkish Proverb

Ice-Cream and Brandied Bananas

Serves 6

6 bananas

juice of ½ lemon

50g butter

3 tablespoons brown sugar

4 tablespoons brandy

juice of 1 orange

vanilla ice-cream, to serve

Peel the bananas, slice lengthwise and squeeze over the lemon juice. Heat the butter in a medium frying pan (non-stick is best). When it sizzles, fry the bananas until lightly browned. Sprinkle with brown sugar, pour over the brandy, and flame.

When the flames subside, pour in the orange juice and cook uncovered over high heat until the syrup thickens deliciously – don't let the bananas get mushy.

To Serve Scoop ice-cream balls into bowls and top with hot brandied bananas. Serve swiftly, before the ice-cream has a chance to melt.

'Time flies like an arrow; fruit flies like a banana.'

Groucho Marx

Old-Fashioned Guava Snow

Serves 6 to 8

1kg (12 to 14) guavas

2 tablespoons castor sugar

125ml off-dry white wine

150g sugar

250ml cream

Peel the guavas. Slice two very finely into a bowl, sprinkle with castor sugar and refrigerate. This will be used later for garnishing. Cut the remaining guavas in half.

Combine the wine and sugar in a large saucepan. Heat, stirring until sugar dissolves, then add the guavas and simmer uncovered for 20 to 30 minutes until tender. Purée the guavas and all the cooking liquid in a blender or food processor, strain into a bowl, and allow to cool. Whip the cream to stiff peaks, fold into the guava and chill in the fridge.

To Serve Spoon the guava snow into glasses or serving bowls with a few slices of guava.

Boozy Nectarines with Hot Orange Sabayon

The chill of the fruit, offset by a piping hot sauce, contrasts deliciously to create an upbeat scenario. If nectarines aren't in season, use berries; about 600g should be sufficient. The sauce doesn't take kindly to waiting about after being prepared, so dash into the kitchen to make it just before serving.

Serves 6

Boozy Nectarines

6 nectarines

2 tablespoons castor sugar

6 tablespoons citrus-based liqueur

Orange Sabayon

3 egg yolks

2 tablespoons castor sugar

4 tablespoons marsala or medium sherry

4 tablespoons orange juice

Boozy Nectarines Peel and stone the nectarines, then slice finely into a bowl. Sprinkle over the castor sugar and liqueur, and toss everything together. Pile into six glasses and chill well in the fridge.

Orange Sabayon Combine the egg yolks, castor sugar, marsala or sherry and orange juice in a double boiler over simmering water, and whisk with a hand-held electric mixer or balloon whisk until the sabayon is thick and frothy. Remove from the heat and continue whisking for a minute or two to cool slightly.

To Serve Spoon the warm sabayon onto the fruit and serve pronto.

'Love – the feeling – is a fruit of love, the verb.' Stephen R. Covey

Tipsy Figs

Serves 4

8 figs

200ml port

2 tablespoons dark rum

2 tablespoons sugar

2 vanilla pods

mascarpone cheese or vanilla ice-cream, to serve

Cut deep crosses into the figs to open them like flowers. Place two in each serving bowl.

Pour the port and rum into a small saucepan with the sugar. Split the vanilla pods and scrape the seeds into the pan; add the pods as well. Heat gently, stirring until the sugar dissolves.

To Serve Pour the hot syrup onto the figs and place a spoonful of mascarpone or scoop of vanilla ice-cream alongside.

'Gratitude is a fruit of great cultivation; you do not find it among gross people.'

Samuel Johnson

Mangoes in Sweet Wine with Almond Crisps

Serves 4

Mangoes in Sweet Wine

500ml bottle sweet wine (late harvest, noble late harvest, straw wine, natural sweet, sauternes)

2 mangoes

Almond Crisps

100g flaked almonds

50g cake flour

50g castor sugar

60ml egg whites

50g butter

Mangoes in Sweet Wine Chill the wine. Skin, stone and slice the mangoes into a bowl, cover and return to the fridge to chill while you're making the almond crisps.

Almond Crisps Lightly oil one large or two smaller baking trays. Heat the oven to 180°C. Pop three-quarters of the almonds into a food processor with the flour and castor sugar and whizz until quite finely crumbled. Whizz in the egg whites and melted butter; don't over-process as the almonds should stay textured.

Drop heaped teaspoonfuls of the biscuit mixture onto the baking tray/s, leaving plenty of space for spreading. Spread evenly into circles and scatter the remaining almonds on top, pressing them gently into the batter. Bake for 7 to 8 minutes. The biscuits should be quite brown around the edges and paler in the centre. Lift onto a cake rack to cool. Store, if necessary, in an airtight container.

To Serve Pour chilled wine into glasses and add mango slices. Place almond crisps alongside.

Panna Cotta with Plum Sauce

If plums aren't in season, use berries in the sauce; or make two different fruit toppings for added interest.

Serves 8

Panna Cotta

4 gelatine leaves

500ml cream

150g castor sugar

500ml plain yoghurt

3 tablespoons amaretto liqueur

Plum Sauce

250g plums

4 tablespoons clear honey

Panna Cotta Soften the gelatine leaves in iced water for a few minutes. Combine the cream, castor sugar and yoghurt in a heatproof bowl over a pan of simmering water and stir until smooth and warm. Squeeze the excess water from the gelatine with your hands, add to cream mixture and stir until the gelatine dissolves. Do not overheat, otherwise the yoghurt will curdle.

Remove from the heat and stir in the liqueur. Pour into eight glasses, cover and refrigerate for about 6 hours until set.

Plum Sauce Cut the plums into chunks and discard the stones. Pop into a blender or food processor with the honey and purée smoothly. Pass through a fine sieve and chill.

To Serve Spoon plum sauce onto the panna cotta. A mint sprig would make a jolly garnish if you think that an extra touch of colour will cheer things up

'The tree of silence bears the fruit of peace.' Arabian Proverb

Chocolate Chilli Shots with Citrus Salad

Serves 8 to 10

Chocolate Chilli Shots

100g dark chocolate, chopped

1 red chilli, seeded and finely chopped

6 egg yolks

1 tablespoon instant coffee granules

2 tablespoons hot water

100g castor sugar

3 tablespoons clear honey

150g unsalted butter, cut into chunks

50g cocoa powder, sifted

250ml cream

Citrus Salad

3 oranges

3 naartjies or satsumas

3 tablespoons castor sugar

2 teaspoons cornflour

Chocolate Chilli Shots Melt the chocolate in a bowl over simmering water. Remove from the heat and beat in the chilli and egg yolks. Dissolve the coffee in hot water, mix in the castor sugar and honey and stir into the chocolate.

Add the butter and cocoa and beat in until well blended. Whip the cream stiffly, and fold in. Pour or pipe into 10 glasses (or 20 shot glasses) and refrigerate for about 4 hours to set.

Citrus Salad Finely grate the zest of one orange. Peel and segment all the oranges and naartjies or satsumas and place in a bowl. Squeeze the juice from the skins and filaments into a medium saucepan and add the orange zest, castor sugar and cornflour. Bring to the boil, stirring until the sugar dissolves. Boil for a minute or two until the sauce is clear and thickened. Mix in the fruit segments and allow the salad to cool.

To Serve Spoon a little citrus salad onto the chocolate chilli shots and serve with small spoons.

Pastries with Peaches and Mascarpone

Serves 6

400g puff pastry

1 egg

1 tablespoon milk

250g mascarpone cheese

3 freestone peaches

2 tablespoons castor sugar

Heat the oven to 200°C. Defrost the pastry, unroll it and cut it into six squares. Place on a lightly oiled baking sheet. Whisk together the egg and milk, and brush a little around the edges of the pastry (offer the rest to the cat).

Spread the mascarpone into the pastries. Peel, core and thinly slice the peaches, then pile the slices onto the mascarpone. Sprinkle evenly with castor sugar.

Bake for 15 to 20 minutes until the pastries are crisp and golden and the peaches are soft and lightly charred. Turn on the oven griller for a few minutes at the end if necessary for extra colour.

To Serve Serve these tarts warm, preferably not too long after they've been baked.

Brie with Figs and Mangoes in Balsamic Syrup

Serves 8

250ml dry white wine

250ml water

2 tablespoons balsamic vinegar

100g sugar

3 star anise

6 slices green ginger (leave the skin on)

250g soft-dried figs

250g soft-dried mango slices

250g ripe brie

crisp biscuits or crusty bread, to serve

Combine the wine, water, balsamic vinegar, sugar, star anise and ginger in a medium saucepan and stir over low heat until the sugar dissolves. Bring the syrup to the boil. Add the figs and mangoes, cover and simmer over very low heat for about 30 minutes until the fruit is lusciously tender.

Uncover and boil briskly until the syrup has reduced and thickened (remember that it will thicken further as it cools). Leave the fruit in the syrup to cool.

To Serve Bring the brie to room temperature before serving, sliced, with the figs and mangoes – and a little of the delish syrup – alongside. Crisp biscuits or sliced crusty bread are great to round things off.

'Fruits that blossom first will first be ripe.'

William Shakespeare

Fruit Index

Recipe Index

Recipe Index